TO ....

From ....

Date ....

Note

Tips To Bring Your Coloring To The Next Level
First of all, pick coloring tools:

You can use pens, markers, pencils, or crayons. Choose whatever you like in terms of texture and feeling. If I would do recommend, here it is. I'd go with pencils for beginner. If you are wanting to play with some advanced techniques or detail work, then go with a set of pencils and a set of markers. Then of course you can throw in pens, crayons, lead pencils, and more later.

Palette/Theme or Better to pick a concept:

Picking color palettes is not easy. I used to spend more than an hours to see professional talk about this. Thus, I recommend making it easier on yourself by using available color palette online. You may search it very easy from Pinterest or use design-seeds website. You will get much more idea to make your artwork great and special.

Finally:

Just do it and let loose. Coloring is an effective stress management and meditation. Let coloring be your calm and have a great

....

Colorist's Name

....

Date

Note

Note

Note

Note

Note

Note

Note

Note

Note

Note

Note

Note

Note

Note

Note

Note

Note

Note

Note

Note

Note

Note

Note

Note

Note